day pulls down the sky

a   filament in   gold leaf

day pulls down the sky © Okwui Okpokwasili
a   filament in   gold leaf © Asiya Wadud

This book has been made possible in part by the New York State Council on the Arts, the Leslie Scalapino - O Books Fund, and donations for individuals. Belladonna* is a proud member of CLMP. Okwui Okpokwasili's *day pull down the sky* is produced by Danspace Project and made possible with lead support from the Howard Gilman Foundation, Lambent Foundation, Doris Duke Charitable Foundation, and the Andrew W. Mellon Foundation.

Distributed to the trade by
Small Press Distribution
1341 Seventh Street
Berkeley, CA 94710
www.SPDBooks.org

Also available directly through

BELLADONNA*
925 Bergen Street, Suite 405
Brooklyn, NY 11238
www.belladonnaseries.org

Danspace
Project
St. Mark's Church
131 East 10th Street
New York, NY 10003
www.danspaceproject.org

a   filament in   gold leaf

asiya wadud

$\oplus$

day pulls down the sky

okwui okpokwasili

This book, *day pulls down the sky / a filament in gold leaf* is comprised of Okwui Okpokwasili's song lyrics and Asiya Wadud's poems written in response to them. These pages contain both a collaboration and two parallel manuscripts, with Wadud's "a filament in gold leaf" heading the pages, and Okpokwasili's lyrics for "day pulls down the sky" footnoted by the musical sign for coda. We selected this sign in order to express the connection between Okpokwasili's lyrics and Wadud's poems. The coda notation indicates "expanded cadence."

In writing through Okpokwasili's music, Wadud wrote poems as she listened to particular songs and wrote the entire suite of poems listening to the album's sixth song, "follow me." The grey scale coda signifies the presence of "follow me" throughout the entirety of *a filament in gold leaf,* and the black coda marks a more singular association between specific poems and songs.

0

a fibonacci builds   around us

we start off with the one
incremental guesswork

all the voids   1x1
all constituent fibrous parts
all around us?
all around us.

1

⊕ a fibonacci builds in a chorus, as filament

          all the numbers building in accordance

          every single smaller number

             requisite scaffolding

a fibonacci builds in a chorus, as filament — all the congregants fervent in the
thickets — all the congregants fervent;   we see them

dust clouds each among us — who has never seen this?
what brews inside the structure? who has never asked them?
what brews inside the structure? who has never heard the noise?
shrouded later in what it contains — dust clouds among us

day pulls down the sky ⊕ It is not that I have no past / Rather it continually fragments on the / Terrible
and vivid ephemera of now / I am / I am the face beneath the sand / Still breathing / While day pulls down
the sky, / While the day pulls down the sky.

and what brews between the structures? [that might be our own secret]

we converged ; & saved space for filament

to pass through and see us   to pass through and name the vacuum

at the start and the finish

it remains attenuated

a fibonacci builds in a chorus — a fibonacci builds in a chorus, then crescendo

    all the congregants fervent in the thickets

    endurance is letting the horse rest when it needs it

    all the congregants fervent in the thickets

all the congregants fervent in the thickets

all the congregants fervent in the thickets

      a testament to all our brokenness

      is everyone fervent among us

      is how we break bread when we have it

      it's split and equally among us

dust clouds each among us — who has never seen this ?
what brews inside the structure? who has never asked them?
double this to build the helix   what would that do
what is among us   why you ask us?   watch it long enough
          and it is apparent   opacity or distance
connective tissue thin strip   all the congregants fervent in the thickets
all the congregants with bare legs
dust brews and then settles
no space was neutral

the space now has a witness — who will witness the dispersal with the same
attention as the accumulation? all the congregants, or bare witness

          observant creatures bear witness   the nocturnes see us

the only fawn bears witness
it told us it would come as witness
feasting on honeydew and when it's full
       it bears witness
       to the space
       to accumulation then dispersal
       to anything that needs a witness
       the fawn said he'd do this

          but first he had to touch the thickets to see why everyone
          was fervent — the haptic as fawnknowledge
          now he understood the bushes

every trophoblast possible logic, look to the sacristy — all my mother's
containment — all my mother's containment nurtured throughout her garden
she built her garden near the congregants so they could feast, too

when the fruit grew she proclaimed: "look what I cultivated despite all this
dispersal look how my garden grew I've been exonerated"

she called it a garden then disclosure — the fruit grew for four seasons. the cycle
didn't rupture that's because she didn't expect it to

      I saw the fawn come to feast on honeydew. My mother didn't
        expect it. The fawn didn't know I saw it — he feasted until he was full and
then he plucked another. a fibonacci builds in a chorus — a fibonacci accumulates
in a chorus ,   grows heavy stretch it out to spread the load — all the congregants
part of honeydew harvest

•

the congregants are on their backs they are looking straight at the sun they like
the orb's directness and how the light enshrouds them   they need
the orb's distance, who doesn't among us? all the light just beyond us — who
doesn't among us?

everysingle one of them
all their vertebra
stretched out   in latitude
to see what is to come
some kind of knowledge

one thing to be sure of
one thing that we can know
is all congregants become the one

is   all   congregants   become   the   one

2

⊕ a noiseless mathematics permeated everything. how the structure built itself took
all parts from its rucksack and stacked them for scaffolding and how the structure
built itself used the sides of other buildings to act as witness to act as juncture to
act as gloved structure or each other

.   a mathematics in its precision a quiet premonition governs us.
as the structure looks at us.   we act as blueprint — stairs in the far corner,
doors that act as windows, windows that structure us to look past containment.
I left the window cracked, I did this on purpose.   anything could get out.
everything could come in.   nothing was ever neutral.   this is something we
know. all that is magnetic at the perimeter — all mathematics a divining and then
the structure does its business   usually it's an ascension
or if not
sutures to build a latitude a throughway to build a road that bleeds out, to build
a road that bleeds

out

sam's song ⊕ I thought the day was a stranger to night / Then there they were / Standing right beside
each other / fingers intertwined / just like grace / wasn't that grace // I ask for grace / Grace / Show me
grace grace // I'm chasing the dawn / And falling headlong into twilight / I hope with grace / in the light
of grace / grace // Even entangled in light / I'm not a stranger to the night / I'm not a stranger tonight /
Could that be grace / Show me grace // I'm chasing the dawn / And falling headlong into twilight / With
some grace / I hope with grace // In the light of grace / Show me grace // I thought the day was a stranger
to night / Then there they were / standing right beside each other / fingers intertwined / isn't that grace?
/ wasn't that grace?

3

⊕ I can only speak of riven things, how elastic their expectation — all the bands
that double back, all the bands that circle back. a little din at my nape
that was to guide us as we drifted that was to direct us back

I can only speak of supplicants
their palms cupped patiently
point to point governs them
how they insist on the whole thing
whether or not it's
broken

broken is a way for
filament
to pass through
any space
for riven things
to double back
and see all the pieces
we line them up in accordance
to their ability to hold any space
little din at my nape
that was to guide us if we drifted

get ahold ⊕   gotta get a hold of me / thought I had a hold of me / gotta get a hold of me / no one got
a hold of me / whose gonna get / who wants a hold of me / hold / I was wondering where you are / is
someone coming for me / someone's gonna come for me / someone's gotta hold of me / hold me

4

one   I made for you a vestment a container in which to keep you
          vestibule rich with lichen and breath   a sharp hole to see past
          — all the rest comes, too

two   I made for you this crescent nail beds filled in the areas where light passes
          but I left it porous, I left it that way — that's for what will pass through
          this is what will pass through

of wishing and superheroes They say there was a time when love was blind / I say that time there never was // That who are they / They are no more / to the victor / Go the spoils // And the most lying li(n)es / Of history-Cause / It was always beautiful / Unlike the terrible now // But I say if then was / As they say it was / How could Now go so astray // So if then was now / And now / Was then / I say both times twice / Left at least a few / Somebodies bent back / Over besides // Bent back far enough / And fit to break // I say back then / There was a rending / A mining / A ruining // Just like now / Just like this time / Maybe now sitting in front of the screen / And behind the screen / All at the same time // Creates a friction / A feeling of multiples / Designed / to make you wretch fetch / Catch a bleary eye / Numb sucked soul sucked / Unmirrored time // You think you can spin the world / Around / Soar up in the sky / You could be flying / Flying blind // Around the whole / Whole round world // Maybe you can take my hand // I will go with you / I will go with you / I will fly I will dive / Head over heals // Into the pool / That is empty / You and me / We will have no feet / We will fly / Round and round // Our bodies / Shape the air like clay in our hands // I say can we make this time that time now / We must make it now the time / To put aside / the lying / We been doing we been doing / It is time / to put aside / the lying / the lying we been doing // we got to remember we got to say what we can about the true pain // we can you can in my hands together we will // we will / we will remember all that time and we will say it was not fine and now / now we will make it so. We will make it so. Now we will make it so. // If I stay asleep / If I count some sheep / If I sink in too deep / Won't I miss the sunlight break / Who will hold me now / As I swing in this bower / Isn't this a late hour / I don't have no cares to shake / But I ——

three   my mouth is full of whatever I put in it and
           what I put there is often red clay, magnolia, okra, cutlass, the
           distance the distance is as long as we see it

four   what next ?   the thin strip
           first my eye , then my eyes
           the other parts a new extension
           all extremities keep on pulling
           all extremities lichen-rich
           all the sealife that grips them
                salted ocean
           first my eye , then my eyes
           — all the rest comes, too

5

⊕ all my evanescence etched in filament— a fact
             you are my isthmus
             you are my bridge
             the throughway that
             shunts everything through
             this

bone cartilage irregular structure
all
33
vertebra — yes, I was counting them
             I counted them to know the structure and to know the distance
             I counted them because its a way to know their containment
             to reach for their comportment

all contiguous land forms — all my evanescence — all congregants become the one
all vertebra acting as ligature
             every disc doing its business

binding song ⊕ I can go for days / Don't tell me to stop / Don't tell me not to go / The thread runs through my navel / Then round and round your waist too / Let me hear you say / I can go for days / Don't tell me to stop / Don't tell me not to go / The thread runs through my navel / Then round and round your waist too / Let me hear you say / Come on, Come on, Come on / Come on, Come on, Come on / I'm irradiated / I'm illuminated / I'm intoxicated / I'm emblazoned / I won't loosen this thread, no / I will wind it tighter / I will bind us closer / I will knot us up / I will wind it tighter / I will bind us closer / I will knot us up / Don't leave a wound tonight...

27

6

⊕ take this hand in the valley
take this hand

take this hand in the valley
take this hand, it's mine

my hands grace the smallest
plants that grow within the valley

my hands near the pinnacle
I bind the plants and dry them

take my hands tenfold
dividend of family

take any organ sequence — disperse
look   at   our   hands, this plain
see what we're given

follow me ⊕   I ask you to follow me / Follow me, follow me, follow me / Through the bush you will wonder
wonder you will wonder / wander / Wonder wander wonder // I tell you what you will see / Restless Spirit
who lost its feet / No one be feeding you / You lost your feet / A mouth talking through its teeth / You are
toes looking for the feet / Who's hand is forcing your defeat / Who's hand is ripping you piece by piece /
All manner of abomination // Restless Spirit who lost its feet / Restless Spirit coming over me / I beg who
are you who am I / I beg who are you who am I / I beg I beg I beg.

laid flat, some   credence
uplift   tenfold
stretched out for governance

all the ecclesiastic eyes
sightline to bear witness

pinhole to bear the valley
all sequencing a principle
of what is a filament
that we come to know then
time grants us this

       in   a   low   valley
      we   look   up

all verdant structures see us
our eyes look to what each distance bears
to see if it will shroud us
all the walls in vestibules they open up like windows

look left to see what
conscriptions
but that's just the congregants

but did you look at their
eyes?
but did you look at them direct?

because what I saw was a filament
brewing
a fibonacci brick by brick
look at the structure's dense jointwork

all the structure's magic rests right at the corners
get up close to see its logic

take some distance to see its sequence
all small parts urgent

a fibonacci builds in a chorus — disperse
marvel at the thread's logic

did you ever see an object reach like this — in a chorus?
did you ever see such enclosed logic ?

the chorus now becomes the throughway
that's when the voices do it justice

look at the long line of all the parts
we lay them out side by side
that was to take stock of them
        then thread them

look at all the parts' quiet accretion
we lay them out side by side
that was because it was stabilizing
to know their governing structures

the sequence built from the corners
organdome
patchwork

the sequence all spooled
each part its own logic

vertebra they work together
and staid

what other sequences keep us ?
what about the adhesions

all the tight cornerwork
brick by brick we built the lattice
talk about an ascension

but then talk about the steady corners

cumulus clouds gather at the setback
cumulus clouds gather as an easement
pushing up against everything
that's their business

7

⊕ At the end of the day everything gathered — little bits of me, my thin follicles.
My eyelash, tender threshold for cornea. My dominance, my sovereignty
spread thin. Thickets thickets for a journey saved for the corner this, we can
call it organdome this part of my body which yokes us. Is this part of me? Is
this also part of me? Which slim filament? Which one did you need? What
once did you need? A space fulfills its new shape with the heaped corner
obfuscating all the amber edges. What we couldn't see in the glass jars — their
lids askew — o, that's to let the air pass through. The corner's right angle widens
by a few degrees — that's to accommodate the expectant girth. All the ancient
cormorants are now circling the towers , the storm petrels follow suit. A
long band of focused birds — birds all along the continuum from filament to
propulsion — that's what I now call a corner. What governs the space are the
angles , a malleable state grips me , the viscous matter spilling out, amber.
The corners were a suggestion so we could decide when to hear them; their
braying and their insistence and their backs are towards us. We all finally turn
from the corners clockwise, we drape the single shroud over all of us, exhaust all
twine to grip us —

exhaust all twine, yoke for yoke.

---

radio⊕ You hear the radio buzz? / Radiation and broken glass / I am like those / broken waves / Particles
of dust / And radiant air now passing through / It's the song that goes on / That would be my wished for
life / To swell and recede / And continue unbroken

8

from
the
thickets
the
cormorants
now
need
just
one
shroud

everyone at rest
everything resplendent
look at the sightline
how it coasts so gently

a   filament   in   gold leaf
a   filament   and salt preserved
a   filament and attenuation
a fibonacci built from a chorus
we are resting on our backs
all the small objects, choral
magnifying their voices, fervent
rock hewn and a requirement
all the minor objects needed for the next breath

Note

day pulls down the sky / a filament in gold leaf marks a first-time collaboration between Belladonna* Collaborative and Danspace Project.

day pulls down the sky is the title of Okpokwasili's first (and simultaneously released) LP initiated by Danspace Project's executive director and chief curator Judy Hussie-Taylor who brought the idea of a recording to Okwui during one of their meetings about Danspace's Platform 2020 and research institute. These songs were written by Okwui between 2012 - 2018 some specifically for her interdisciplinary performances. Four of the songs were first performed by Okwui at Danspace Project, including "sam's song" on the occasion of Sam Miller's memorial on September 15, 2018. They were recorded on January 8, 2019 at the studio of recording engineer John Kilgore. The album was produced by Okwui's longtime artistic collaborator Peter Born.

Immediately upon hearing about this recording, Belladonna's founder Rachel Levitsky had the idea to publish the lyrics and to invite Asiya Wadud to write in response to Okwui's songs.

Song Credits

day pulls down the sky
    words by Samuel R. Delany and David Wojnarowicz
    song by Okwui Okpokwasili
    piano by Peter Born

sam's song
    words and song by Okwui Okpkwasili
    music by Peter Born

get ahold
    song by Okwui Okpokwasili

of wishing and superheroes
    words by Okwui Okpokwasili
    song by Okwui Okpokwasili and Umechi Born

binding song
    words and song by Okwui Okpokwasili
    music by Peter Born

follow me
    words, song and music by Okwui Okpokwasili

radio
    words and song by Okwui Okpokwasili

Danspace Project

Danspace Project presents new work in dance, supports a diverse range of choreographers in developing their work, encourages experimentation, and connects artists to audiences.

For over 40 years, Danspace Project has supported a vital community of contemporary dance artists in an environment unlike any other in the United States. Located in the historic St. Mark's Church in-the-Bowery, Danspace shares its facility with the Church, The Poetry Project, and New York Theatre Ballet. Danspace Project's Commissioning Initiative has commissioned over 570 new works since its inception in 1994.

Danspace Project's Choreographic Center Without Walls (CW²) provides context for audiences and increased support for artists. Our public programs (including Danspace Presents, Platforms, Food for Thought, DraftWork), Commissioning Initiative, residencies, guest artist curators, and contextualizing activities and materials are core components of CW² offering a responsive framework for artists' works. Since 2010, we have produced twelve Platforms, published twelve print catalogues and five e-books, launched the Conversations Without Walls discussion series, and explored models for public discourse and residencies.

Special Thanks to Danspace Project Staff and Board of Directors.

Belladonna* Collaborative

2019 marks the 20th anniversary of the Belladonna* mission to promote the work of women* and feminist writers who are adventurous, experimental, politically involved, multi-form, multicultural, multi-gendered, impossible to define, unpredictable, and dangerous with language. Belladonna* is committed to publishing and building literary community among women-identified and LGBTQIA+ authors who write off-center, producing work that is political and critical; situational rather than plot-driven; inter-subjective, performative, or witnessing; work that reaches across the boundaries and binaries of literary genre and artistic fields, and that questions the gender binary.

Okwui Okpokwasili

Okwui Okpokwasili is a Brooklyn-based multidisciplinary artist. Her work includes two Bessie Award winning productions: *Pent-Up: a revenge dance* and *Bronx Gothic*, which premiered at Danspace Project and was co-commissioned by Performance Space New York (formerly PS 122). Other performance works include *Poor People's TV Room* and *Adaku's Revolt*. Okpokwasili is a 2018 Doris Duke Awardee and a 2018 MacArthur Foundation Fellow.

Asiya Wadud

Asiya Wadud is the author of *Crosslight for Youngbird*, published by Nightboat Books in 2018. Her book *Syncope* (Ugly Duckling Presse) is forthcoming later in 2019, and *No Knowledge Is Complete Until It Passes Through My Body* will be out in 2020. She teaches poetry at Saint Ann's School and leads an English conversation class for new immigrants at the Brooklyn Public Library. She lives in Brooklyn, New York.